Across Five A...

L-I-T *Guide*
Literature In Teaching

By Irene Hunt

A Study Guide for Grades 5 and Up

Prepared by Charlotte S. Jaffe & Barbara T. Doherty

Illustrated by Karen Neulinger

ISBN 1-56644-975-8

© 1995 Educational Impressions, Inc., Hawthorne, NJ

EDUCATIONAL IMPRESSIONS, INC.
Hawthorne, NJ 07507

Printed in the United States.

This study guide is based on the book *Across Five Aprils:*
  Copyright 1964 by Irene Hunt
  Published by Berkley Books: New York.

Across Five Aprils
Written by Irene Hunt

STORY SUMMARY

It is 1861 and a time of great conflict for the Creighton family, who live just outside of Newton, a town in southern Illinois. The children of Matt and Ellen Creighton are divided in their loyalties to the Union. Nine-year-old Jethro does not fully understand the political debate, but is caught up in the excitement, confusion, and anxiety. When the Confederates attack Fort Sumter and the Civil War begins, John and Tom Creighton and cousin Eb quickly sign up to fight on the Union side; Bill Creighton joins the Confederate Army. Shadrach Yale, a local school teacher and romantic interest of Jenny Creighton, helps Jeth follow the progress of the war and the whereabouts of the family members until he, too, is called to duty on the side of the Union.

Because of his brothers' absence and his father's illness, Jethro is forced to assume more of the responsibility for the family farm. Matt Creighton decides to allow Jeth to drive to town alone with the wagon and a team of horses—a difficult task for such a young boy. In Newton, Jeth encounters resentment from some of the townspeople, angered because Jeth's brother Bill has joined the Confederate cause. The hostility later erupts, resulting in the destruction of the Creightons' barn by arson.

Other problems plague the family: They receive news that Tom has been killed in battle. They also learn that Shad has been seriously wounded. Cousin Eb, who has deserted his regiment, suddenly appears at their home, and Jeth does not know whether to turn him in or to help him.

The Civil War slowly comes to a close with fierce fighting on both sides. Finally, the Confederates can hold out no longer. Terms of peace are signed at Appomattox Court House in Virginia. The great joy of peace is tempered, however, by the cruel news of the assassination of President Lincoln.

Life goes on for the Creighton family, but with some changes. Jethro, now matured, reluctantly makes plans to leave the farm. He will live with Shad and Jenny, now married, in order to improve his future by bettering his education.

Meet the Author
Irene Hunt

Books and education were always of great value to Irene Hunt. As a teacher and writer, Ms. Hunt believed that children are more willing to accept a message told in a good book than from an adult. "Books bring new dimensions of happiness, of confidence, and enlightenment to young people from the age of three up," she once noted.

Irene Hunt was born outside of Newton, Illinois, on May 18, 1907. She spent her childhood on the family farm, which she used as the setting for her first novel, *Across Five Aprils*. Her second novel and winner of the Newbery Award, *Up the Road Slowly*, was also based upon childhood memories: Her father had died when she was still a young girl. When a friend asked her, "You're not going to live here anymore, are you?" the troubled Irene hid in a closet. She used this recollection in the novel.

Across Five Aprils received great critical recognition. It was published in 1964 when the author was fifty-seven years old. It won many awards, including the Lewis Carroll Shelf Award and the Charles Follett Award, and it was a Newbery Medal Honor Book. This book, set in the Civil War period, required extensive historical research. The fictional part of the story about the Creighton family, however, was based on the author's family records and letters as well as stories told to her by her grandfather.

Other children's books written by Irene Hunt include *A Trail of Apple Blossoms* and *No Promises in the Wind.*

Pre-Reading Activity
Civil War Beginnings

The Civil War, one of the bloodiest wars in American history, began in 1861 and ended in 1865. By the time Abraham Lincoln became President, trouble had already started. The North and the South were divided on many issues, among them slavery. The southern states wanted to preserve slavery in order to support their economic way of life. The northern states, on the other hand, wanted to end slavery and to turn to a more industrialized economy. The northerners wanted change, and the southerners were content with the way things were.

The Civil War is also known as the War Between the States. Even before Abraham Lincoln had been sworn in as President of the United States of America, seven states had seceded from the Union: Alabama, Florida, Georgia, Louisiana, Mississippi, South Carolina, and Texas. These states formed the Confederate States of America and elected Jefferson Davis as President. On April 12, 1861, Confederate troops fired on Union soldiers stationed at Fort Sumter, South Carolina. The Civil War officially began. Four more states seceded from the Union: Arkansas, North Carolina, Tennessee, and Virginia. Part of Virginia, however, remained loyal to the Union; it became West Virginia and officially joined the Union in 1863.

The United States Divided

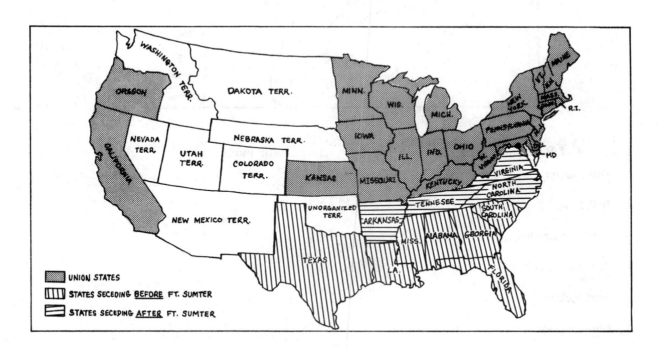

1. After Fort Sumter, how many states had left the Union? _____

2. After Fort Sumter, how many states were in the Union? _____

Across Five Aprils 5

Pre-Reading Activity
Major Battles of the Civil War

The firing on Fort Sumter marked the beginning of the war. This and the other battles listed below are discussed in *Across Five Aprils.* As you read about each in the story, write down a few facts related to the battle. Include when the battle occurred, which side won, the generals in charge, and other important facts.

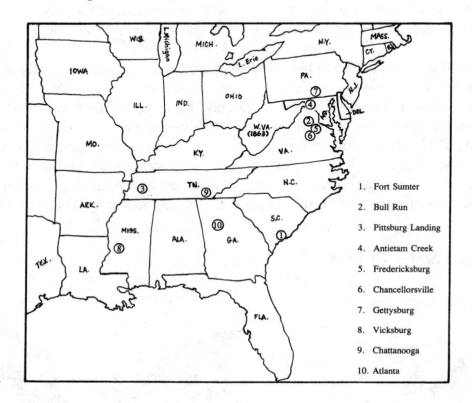

1. Fort Sumter
2. Bull Run
3. Pittsburg Landing
4. Antietam Creek
5. Fredericksburg
6. Chancellorsville
7. Gettysburg
8. Vicksburg
9. Chattanooga
10. Atlanta

Location of Battle   **Important Facts**

1. Fort Sumter

2. Bull Run

3. Pittsburg Landing

4. Antietam Creek

5. Fredericksburg

6. Chancellorsville

7. Gettysburg

8. Vicksburg

9. Chattanooga

10. Atlanta

Vocabulary
Chapter One

Use the words in the box to complete the sentences below. You may need to use your dictionary.

accustomed	alleged	aloof	amiable	apathy
caress	coveted	destiny	exasperate	dissipate
imminence	melancholy	perplexities	persecuted	physics
radiance	secession	shiftless	tariffs	typhoid

1. Even after weeks of winter, Bob wasn't _____ to the cold.

2. It was his _____ to become a great leader.

3. The _____ child got along with everyone.

4. The doctor felt _____ because so many died from _____ fever.

5. Mom touched the baby's head with a gentle _____ while she sang.

6. The _____ of the battle caused a great deal of apprehension.

7. The _____ of the sun seemed to _____ as the day progressed.

8. It was _____ that the general was _____ and indifferent.

9. Eleven states voted for _____ from the Union.

10. Andrew did not seem to care about his work; his _____ worried his teacher.

11. He learned about gravity, magnetism, and other phenomena in _____ class.

12. _____ upon imported goods were a cause for disagreement.

Five of the vocabulary words from the first part of this activity were not used. Write an original sentence for each.

_____

_____

_____

_____

_____

Comprehension and Discussion Questions
Chapter One

Answer the following questions in complete sentence form. Give examples from the story to support your response.

1. Describe Jethro's feelings about war. Do you think he had a mature, realistic vision of war? Explain.

_____

_____

_____

_____

2. Shad left for Newton in the midst of a late planting season, supposedly to get needed supplies for Matt. What was the real reason for leaving the farm during such a busy time?

_____

_____

_____

3. How did Jethro compare his feelings toward his father with those he had for President Lincoln?

_____

_____

_____

4. The author used foreshadowing in this chapter by hinting that Bill's views about the impending war might differ from those of his brothers: ''And Bill, for the first time that John could remember, had reservations about a subject and seemed unwilling to discuss it with his brother.'' Use this to predict a decision that Bill will make in a later chapter.

_____

_____

_____

_____

Vocabulary
Chapter Two

Use your dictionary to define the following words as they were used in the chapter.

1. abolitionist

2. assailant

3. coal-oil

4. din

5. downtrodden

6. festering

7. gravely

8. grieve

9. hypocrite

10. industrialist

11. pious

12. politics

13. rebel

14. strident

15. tremulous

16. winced

An Acrostic

An acrostic is a poem or series of lines in which the first letter of each line forms a word or words. Usually, the lines have something to do with the word or words that are being spelled. The following is an example of an acrostic:

APRIL

A braham Lincoln

P lanting

R umors flowing

I llinois divided

L ooking towards war

Now create your own acrostic poem. Use one of the following titles as the basis or choose your own: Civil War, Lincoln, Slavery, or Farming. You must use at least six vocabulary words from the first part of this activity; however, the words do not have to come at the beginning of the lines.

Comprehension and Discussion Questions
Chapter Two

Answer the following questions in complete sentence form. Give examples from the story to support your response.

1. How did Wilse try to justify the fact that he owned slaves?

_____

_____

_____

_____

2. How have Jethro's feelings toward war changed?

_____

_____

_____

_____

3. Chart Wilse's, John's, and Bill's positions on the issue of war between the North and the South. Find at least one statement made by each character that shows which side he will probably be on should war occur.

_____

_____

_____

_____

4. What important news did Shadrack bring to the family? Explain its importance.

_____

_____

_____

_____

Vocabulary
Chapter Three

Match the vocabulary words on the left to the definitions on the right. Place the correct letter on each line.

_____ 1. abide

_____ 2. awed

_____ 3. bayonet

_____ 4. blithely

_____ 5. chafed

_____ 6. eloquence

_____ 7. inflamed

_____ 8. oratory

_____ 9. prestige

_____ 10. pursuit

_____ 11. quaver

_____ 12. sullen

_____ 13. tedium

_____ 14. turmoil

_____ 15. wastrel

_____ 16. whim

_____ 17. wrath

A. annoyed; worn away

B. art of public speaking

C. influential status

D. act of chasing

E. quality of being tiresome or uninteresting

F. happily; lightheartedly

G. one who uses resources foolishly

H. to wait patiently; to withstand

I. persuasive and fluent expression

J. sulky; resentful

K. strong, resentful anger

L. filled with dread, wonder, and reverence

M. a rifle with knife blade attached

N. sudden idea

O. excited to strong emotion

P. extreme confusion or agitation

Q. tremble

Choose any three vocabulary words from the first part of this activity. Write an original sentence for each.

_____

_____

_____

_____

_____

Comprehension and Discussion Questions
Chapter Three

Answer the following questions in complete sentence form. Give examples from the story to support your response.

1. Why did every weekend seem like a Fourth of July celebration?

_____

_____

_____

_____

2. What change in attitude did Jethro notice after the Battle of Bull Run?

_____

_____

_____

_____

3. How did Jethro's visit to Walnut Hill differ from previous visits?

_____

_____

_____

_____

4. What shocking news did Bill have for Jethro? Why did Jethro hide his face as Bill walked away?

_____

_____

_____

_____

Vocabulary
Chapter Four

Choose the word in each set that is **most like** the first word in meaning.

1. **admonitions:** experiments   warnings   habits

2. **allusion:** magic   portion   hint

3. **balefully:** artificially   comically   ominously

4. **dispel:** scatter   recycle   report

5. **maneuver:** manipulate   approach   malfunction

6. **mimicry:** sorrowful   imitation   puppetry

7. **paisley:** swampy   a flower   swirled pattern

8. **pompous:** spongy   self-important   afraid

9. **rebuke:** remind   report   reprimand

10. **scorn:** injure   wonderful   contempt

11. **skepticism:** doubt   characteristic   scientific

12. **soberly:** safely   seriously   importantly

13. **sympathetic:** compassionate   emphatic   joyous

14. **timidly:** shyly   sleepy   colorful

Comprehension and Discussion Questions
Chapter Four

Answer the following questions in complete sentence form. Give examples from the story to support your response.

1. Why did the bells ring in every city and town in the North?

_____

_____

_____

_____

2. What did Mrs. Creighton ask Jethro to do that improved Jethro's mood after the letter from Tom?

_____

_____

_____

_____

3. Explain what Shad meant when he said, "Thou too, Brutus?"

_____

_____

_____

_____

4. What plan did Shad have for Jethro's future? What advice did he give to Jethro?

_____

_____

_____

_____

Vocabulary
Chapter Five

Use your dictionary to define the following words and phrases as they were used in the chapter.

1. astute

2. belligerently

3. bustle

4. confident

5. county seat

6. exhilarated

7. fare

8. forte

9. indistinct

10. invariably

11. keener

12. loathing

13. oblige

14. pallor

15. passel

16. peered

17. sinister

18. wryly

To Tell the Truth

Using the vocabulary words from the first part of this activity, play "To Tell the Truth." After you and your classmates have located the meanings of the vocabulary words, divide into teams. Each team should be assigned an equal number of the words. Each team will present in turn two incorrect definitions and one true definition for each word. The opposing team or teams will be challenged to select the correct meanings. Be as clever as possible in trying to trick your opponents!

Comprehension and Discussion Questions
Chapter Five

Answer the following questions in complete sentence form. Give examples from the story to support your response.

1. Why did Jethro feel good about being sent to Newton to get food and supplies?

_____

_____

_____

_____

2. Why, do you think, did the editor invite Jethro to dinner? What treasure did he give to Jethro?

_____

_____

_____

_____

3. Guess why Dave Burdow accompanied Jethro on his journey.

_____

_____

_____

_____

4. Why did Jethro hesitate to tell his family about Guy Wortman and the others? Judge Jethro's decision to tell his family all that occurred at the store and on the way home.

_____

_____

_____

_____

Vocabulary
Chapter Six

Use your dictionary to define the following words. Then use the words and their definitions to create a crossword puzzle.

1. allayed

2. amended

3. astonishment

4. arsonist

5. casing

6. chagrin

7. curt

8. evident

9. fervent

10. fret

11. gracious

12. imposed

13. malice

14. omen

15. prophecy

16. raucous

17. subtly

18. tranquil

Create a Crossword Puzzle

Use the vocabulary words (or forms of the words) from the first part of this activity to create a crossword puzzle. Try to use all of them! Number the boxes horizontally and vertically. Darken the boxes that you are not using. Exchange with a classmate to solve!

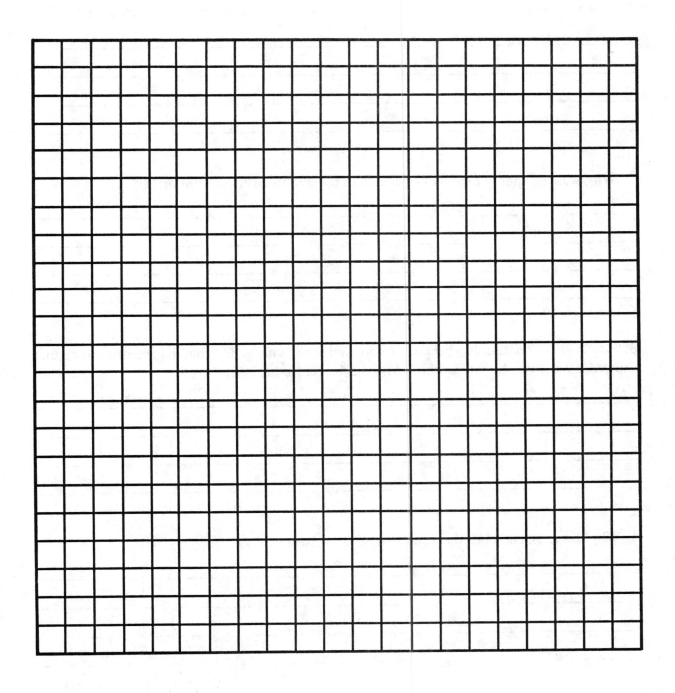

Comprehension and Discussion Questions
Chapter Six

Answer the following questions in complete sentence form. Give examples from the story to support your response.

1. In what ways—other than physical—did Matt Creighton change after his collapse?

_____

_____

_____

_____

2. Why was the family especially anxious to receive word from Tom or Eb?

_____

_____

_____

_____

3. How had the relationship between Jethro and Jenny changed? What did she offer to do that showed how close she felt to him? Why did he refuse her offer?

_____

_____

_____

_____

4. Why did arsonists burn down the Creightons' barn?

_____

_____

_____

_____

Vocabulary
Chapter Seven

Match the vocabulary words on the left to the definitions on the right. Place the correct letter on each line.

_____ 1. acquaintance   A.   boisterous merriment

_____ 2. desperado   B.   basic part of a thing

_____ 3. entrenchments   C.   event or occurrence

_____ 4. essence   D.   situation suited to one's abilities

_____ 5. hilarity   E.   without compassion; cruel

_____ 6. incident   F.   coming after; succeeding

_____ 7. inept   G.   dugouts in banks of earth

_____ 8. integrity   H.   adequately

_____ 9. niche   I.   person known to you

_____ 10. plaudits   J.   mocking remark

_____ 11. ruthless   K.   act of getting even

_____ 12. sarcasm   L.   expressions of praise

_____ 13. subsequent   M.   awkward; clumsy

_____ 14. sufficiently   N.   honesty; sincerity

_____ 15. vengeance   O.   reckless criminal

Story Sentences

Choose any five vocabulary words from the first part of this activity. Use them to write original sentences that tell about events in this book.

_____

_____

_____

_____

_____

_____

_____

Comprehension and Discussion Questions
Chapter Seven

Answer the following questions in complete sentence form. Give examples from the story to support your response.

1. Evaluate the way that the Creightons learned the news about Tom. Do you think a more official way would have been better? Explain your reasoning.

_____

_____

_____

_____

2. Why did the dates in the Bible ''stare up at Jethro with terrible significance'' on that day?

_____

_____

_____

_____

3. Why did Halleck's victory at Corinth seem to be an empty one?

_____

_____

_____

_____

4. According to Jethro, what was the North's main problem?

_____

_____

_____

_____

Vocabulary
Chapter Eight

Use your dictionary to define the following words and phrases as they were used in the chapter.

1. agony

2. anxiety

3. appalling

4. dismay

5. emerged

6. genially

7. intention

8. inevitably

9. incompetence

10. perception

11. plummeted

12. obscurity

13. reclaim

14. reinforcements

Send a Letter

Imagine that you are a soldier fighting in the Civil War. Write a letter home to your friends and family describing the events and your feelings about the war. Use at least eight vocabulary words from the first part of this activity in your letter.

Comprehension and Discussion Questions
Chapter Eight

Answer the following questions in complete sentence form. Give examples from the story to support your response.

1. What was the chilling news that Jethro learned about the war's progress? Why was this news surprising?

_____

_____

_____

_____

2. Why did Ross Milton smile when Jethro corrected his statement ''I allow to get thanks''?

_____

_____

_____

_____

3. What is your opinion of General McClellan after reading Shad's letter?

_____

_____

_____

_____

4. How did Shad view General Burnside and the Battle of Fredericksburg?

_____

_____

_____

_____

Vocabulary
Chapter Nine

Use the words in the box to complete the sentences below. You may need to use your dictionary.

ancestral	bachelor	conscience	credence
decline	deserters	despairing	dodge
faltering	gangrenous	insistence	kerosene
preoccupation	suspicion	triumphant	ventured

1. The soon-to-be-married man was given a _____ party.

2. An honest person is usually above _____.

3. The baby took a few _____ steps, but soon gained more confidence.

4. The candidate worried because the poll showed a _____ in his popularity.

5. The _____ Little League team was treated to ice cream by their joyful coach.

6. When her grandparents died, Joan inherited the _____ home.

7. Don't give any _____ to the rumors you hear!

8. Does your _____ bother you when you tell a lie?

9. Frank _____ down a new path in the forest hoping to find unusual animals.

10. The _____ soldier spoke sadly about the loss of his friends.

11. The soldier's infected wound became _____.

12. My teacher's _____ upon proper grammar helped me improve my writing.

Four of the vocabulary words from the first part of this activity were not used. Write an original sentence for each.

_____

_____

_____

_____

_____

Comprehension and Discussion Questions
Chapter Nine

Answer the following questions in complete sentence form. Give examples from the story to support your response.

1. Who was Hig Phillips? How did he avoid the draft? Why was he murdered? Do you think he deserved his fate? Explain.

_____

_____

_____

_____

2. What was Jenny's attitude toward the men from the Federal Registrars? Did she have a valid reason for her feelings? What would you have done in her place?

_____

_____

_____

_____

3. What were Jeth's considerations in deciding whether or not to help Eb? How did he solve his dilemma?

_____

_____

_____

_____

4. Judge President Lincoln's decision regarding deserters.

_____

_____

_____

_____

Vocabulary
Chapter Ten

An **analogy** is a similarity in some details between things that are otherwise unlike. Solve the following word analogies by using vocabulary from the word box. You may need to use your dictionary.

advantaged	arrogant	conspiracy	contemptuous
dreary	inept	maneuvered	monotonous
optimism	seize	spinster	verified

1. Pleasure is to pain as _____ is to underprivileged.

2. Kind is to caring as conceited is to _____.

3. Peaceful is to warlike as exciting is to _____.

4. Male is to bachelor as female is to _____.

5. _____ is to pessimism as abundant is to meager.

6. Harmful is to injurious as dismal is to _____.

7. Plan is to _____ as crime is to murder.

8. _____ is to grab as bestow is to give.

9. Navigated is to _____ as ceased is to discontinued.

10. Content is to unhappy as _____ is to honorable.

11. _____ is to confirmed as stimulated is to invigorated.

12. Incompetent is to _____ as disaster is to catastrophe.

On the Homefront
How had life changed for the people living at home during the Civil War? Write your impressions in a paragraph that uses at least five vocabulary words from the first part of this activity.

Comprehension and Discussion Questions
Chapter Ten

Answer the following questions in complete sentence form. Give examples from the story to support your response.

1. Why was Joe Hooker's defeat at Chancellorsville so ominous for the Union side?

_____

_____

_____

_____

2. Contrast the public's attitude toward General Grant and toward General Lee.

_____

_____

_____

_____

3. Ross Milton helped the Creightons deal with a crisis. Explain. Do you think Matt would have permitted Jenny to go alone? Discuss your reasons.

_____

_____

_____

_____

4. How did Jenny adapt to life in Washington? Give specific examples to support your opinion.

_____

_____

_____

_____

Vocabulary
Chapter Eleven

Write your own definitions for these vocabulary words. Then look up the definitions in the dictionary. Compare the results!

Word	Your Definition	Dictionary
1. amnesty		
2. betrayal		
3. corruption		
4. desolation		
5. jubilation		
6. mercy		
7. obscurity		
8. pandemonium		
9. proclamation		
10. prominence		
11. reversal		
12. vindictiveness		

You Are There!

Pretend that you are a TV reporter on the scene during a Civil War battle! Do a You Are There account of the events. Interview a soldier or a general. Use at least five vocabulary words from the first part of this activity.

Comprehension and Discussion Questions
Chapter Eleven

Answer the following questions in complete sentence form. Give examples from the story to support your response.

1. According to John, what was the importance of the Battle of Chattanooga?

_____

_____

_____

_____

2. What caused Matt to exclaim tearfully, "Never hev I loved him so much"?

_____

_____

_____

_____

3. Why was Shad's reaction to the nomination of George McClellan mixed?

_____

_____

_____

_____

4. John's letter carried news "that those at home had almost despaired of hearing." Why was it important that Bill had not been at Pittsburg Landing?

_____

_____

_____

_____

Vocabulary
Chapter Twelve

Alphabetize the vocabulary words in the word box below. Then use your dictionary to define the words according to their use in the story.

feat	mockery	vaguely	comprehension
distorted	enraged	delinquent	prairie
gallant	irreparable	serenity	tenacity
abolished	atrocities	congregated	assassination

Picture This

Draw a picture that illustrates an event from this chapter. Beneath the picture write a paragraph explaining what is happening. Use at least five vocabulary words from the first part of this activity.

_____

_____

_____

_____

_____

Comprehension and Discussion Questions
Chapter Twelve

Answer the following questions in complete sentence form. Give examples from the story to support your response.

1. Describe the reaction to General Sherman's march through Georgia. Why was it mixed?

_____

_____

_____

_____

2. "It's a terr'ble thing, it's a pitiful thing, but it's war. The sooner we make one great swoop, the sooner the sufferin' is over." "There be limits even in war. This was mean, mad destruction." Choose one of these statements and explain why you agree or disagree.

_____

_____

_____

_____

3. Explain these two statements made by Ross Milton: "Don't expect peace to be a perfect pearl, Jeth." "It's a far star . . . a dim pinpoint of light in the darkness."

_____

_____

_____

_____

4. Why did the author write, "It was the saddest and most cruel April of the five"?

_____

_____

_____

_____

Spotlight Literary Skill
Compare and Contrast

In your readings, you often will notice similarities and differences among characters, settings, and events. Sometimes you will be asked to compare and contrast; in other words, you will be asked to examine the likenesses and differences of two or more people, places, ideas, or things. **Contrast** always emphasizes differences. **Compare** may focus on likenesses alone or on likenesses and differences.

In this activity, you are challenged to compare and contrast characters from *Across Five Aprils* using a Venn Diagram. A **Venn Diagram** uses circles and ellipses to represent relations between sets. Choose any two characters from the story. List their differences on the outer parts of the circles. List their similarities in the center. Write each character's name on the line above the appropriate section of the diagram.

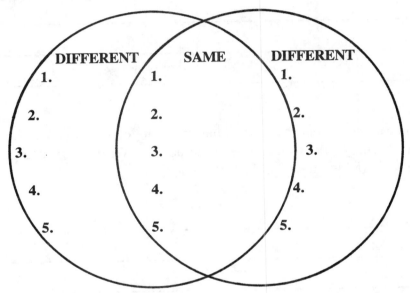

As an added challenge, create another Venn Diagram. Use it to compare and contrast yourself with a story character.

Spotlight Literary Skill
Making Conversation: Dialogue

Dialogue, the spoken words of the characters, is an important feature of most types of writing. In *Across Five Aprils* the characters seem to come alive when we hear them speak to each other. Through dialogue we learn more about how each character thinks, feels, and relates to others. The use of dialogue allows the readers to feel present at the scene of the action.

There are many good examples of realistic dialogue in this story. Write five of your favorites.

_____

_____

_____

_____

_____

_____

Now select two characters from the story. Imagine what you might say to each one if you had the opportunity. Perhaps you would give some advice! Write your dialogue in the spaces below. Be sure to start each new speaker on a new line!

Conversation with _____

_____

_____

_____

_____

_____

Conversation with _____

_____

_____

_____

_____

_____

Spotlight Literary Skill
Mood

Mood is the feeling or effect that is created by the author's words. Settings, actions, characterizations, and descriptions can all be written to convey certain moods. Read the following story selections and think about how the passages make you feel.

On the line below each selection, describe the mood that the author has created:

1. "But on the last Sunday of that April, a Sunday of sunlight and bright sky, Jethro lay in the grass on Walnut Hill, and rage mingled with the grief in his heart. 'Why did it happen? Why—why—did it have to happen?' He lay with his face close to the earth, clutching the fresh spring grass with both hands."

_____

2. "That night there was a great display of fireworks, and then the town's band played while nearly a thousand voices joined in singing 'The Battle Hymn of the Republic.' Jethro's heart swelled in his breast."

_____

3. "But the fall of General Hooker was of little importance compared to the fact that seventeen thousand Union soldiers had gone either to their deaths or to a Confederate prison camp....Was Shadrach Yale one of the seventeen thousand?"

_____

4. "Jethro stood quite still. 'Hello,' he called finally. 'What is it you want of me?' There was no answer....Jethro walked closer, his gun raised, and after a minute, the human voice which he had been half expecting to hear called out to him."

_____

5. "A little distance up the road...Jenny stood at the gate, waiting for them....Her arms were held out to Jethro, and for that moment when he ran toward her, all the shadows were lifted from the April morning."

_____

Spotlight Literary Skill
Characterization

How would you describe Jethro Creighton, the main character in *Across Five Aprils?* Think about his appearance, personality, and actions. On each line below, write a word that defines Jethro. Beneath the line give an example from the book that illustrates the character trait you have provided. A sample is given.

Brave

In Chapter 5 Jethro calmly took the team to Newton. "Jethro maintained the stoic calm...as the wagon swayed....The physical dangers of the road...he could meet calmly, but his heart pounded as he looked toward the Burdow place."

Cooperative Learning Activity
Creating Chapter Titles

The twelve chapters of *Across Five Aprils* are untitled. Discuss the highlights of each chapter with members of your group and brainstorm ideas for original titles. Write the final choice for each chapter in the left column. Give your reasons for each choice on the right. Compare your results with those of the other groups in the class.

TITLES	*Reasons for Choice*
Chapter 1	
Chapter 2	
Chapter 3	
Chapter 4	
Chapter 5	
Chapter 6	
Chapter 7	
Chapter 8	
Chapter 9	
Chapter 10	
Chapter 11	
Chapter 12	

Cooperative Learning Activity
Letter to the Editor

Letters to the editor of a newspaper are usually persuasive and opinionated. In this activity, you are to put yourself in the place of a neighbor of the Creightons. You have just learned of the attack on the Creighton farm and decide to write a letter to the editor. Your letter should include facts describing the incident as well as your feelings about what occurred.

Dear Editor:

With your cooperative learning group, brainstorm other issues that might be the subject of a letter to the editor.

Collect samples of letters to the editor from magazines and newspapers.

Spotlight Literary Skill
Historical Fiction

Historical fiction is a type of writing in which true facts are mixed with fiction. These imaginative stories often include real names, dates, and historical settings to make the tale seem more true to life.

Across Five Aprils is an example of historical fiction. In this activity you are asked to separate the fact from the fiction found in this story. On the left, make a list of historically true facts. On the right, make a list of fictional occurrences in the story. An example of each is given.

HISTORICAL FACTS	FICTIONAL FACTS
1. The Confederates fired on Fort Sumter.	1. Jethro drove the team to Newton.

Post-Reading Activity
What Happened Next?

Create a sequel to the story you have just read. Did Shad return to teaching in Illinois? Did Jethro complete his education? What did he study? What became of Bill? Did he remain estranged from his family? What happened to John and Nancy and their children?

Write your story ideas on another sheet of paper. Try to expand your ideas! You might want to discuss your expansion ideas with your teacher. After you've made corrections and additions, write your finished story here. Use additional paper if necessary.

Perhaps you'd like to illustrate your story!

More Post-Reading Activities

1. How can Jethro's experiences be of value to you in your own life? Use your evaluation skills.

2. In this story, Jethro faced many problems. Choose one situation and tell how you might have handled it differently.

3. With your cooperative learning group, choose a favorite part of the story. Write a script and present your skit to classmates or another class.

4. Study actual poster ads. Then create a poster advertising this book. Remember, the ad should be designed to entice someone to read or buy the book.

5. Find out if there are any Civil War battlefields, monuments, battle re-enactments, or exhibitions in your area. Obtain as much information about them as possible. Which one would you most like to visit? Why?

6. Suppose you had the opportunity to interview Jethro. Think of at least three questions you would like to ask him.

7. Imagine that you are Jethro. Write a diary of your daily thoughts, hopes, and fears. Also record your impressions of the other story characters.

8. Divide into small research groups. Each group will choose a famous person mentioned in the book and gather information about that person. Present your findings in the form of a report to the class. If possible, include a photograph or a sketch. The following are some possible subjects: Henry Ward Beecher, General Bragg, John Brown, Jefferson Davis, William Lloyd Garrison, General Ulysses S. Grant, Wendell Phillips, General George B. McClellan, General ''Stonewall'' Jackson, General Robert E. Lee, Abraham Lincoln, and General William Sherman.

9. Jethro makes a great effort to improve his grammar. Find examples from the story that show how his grammar improves as the story progresses.

10. Create your own historical fiction story! Choose a favorite setting for it. Add many imaginative facts! Before you begin to write your story, list at least ten historical facts about the period you have chosen. You may look in a reference book to find information about this time period. Use these facts as well as knowledge you already possess as background for your story.

Crossword Puzzle
Across Five Aprils

See how much you remember about *Across Five Aprils!* Have fun!

Across

7. Civil War began with Confederate attack here.
8. Type of fiction.
10. John, Tom, and Eb fought on this side.
11. Eb was one.
13. Granted to deserters who returned to service.
15. Left with Shad and Jenny at end of story.
16. Spoken words of the characters.
17. Killed during the Battle of Pittsburg Landing.
19. Author of *Across Five Aprils.*
22. Helped Jethro get through the woods.
23. _____ wrote about Chattanooga.
24. Where treaty was signed.
25. Where Lincoln delivered famous speech.

Down

1. Bill became one.
2. Where Creighton family lived.
3. Hero of Vicksburg.
4. Dugouts in banks of earth.
5. President during Civil War.
6. Wanted to end slavery.
9. Leader of Confederate Army.
12. Jenny became this in Washington, D.C.
14. Schoolmaster who married Jenny.
18. Marched his soldiers through Georgia.
20. Hig Phillips paid to avoid this.
21. Ross Milton's job.

Glossary of Literary Terms

Alliteration: A repetition of initial, or beginning, sounds in two or more consecutive or neighboring words.

Analogy: A comparison based upon the resemblance in some particular ways between things that are otherwise unlike.

Anecdote: A short account of an interesting, amusing or biographical occurrence.

Anticlimax: An event that is less important than what occurred before it.

Archaic language: Language that was once common in a particular historic period but which is no longer commonly used.

Cause and effect: The relationship in which one condition brings about another condition as a direct result. The result, or consequence, is called the effect.

Character development: The ways in which the author shows how a character changes as the story proceeds.

Characterization: The method used by the author to give readers information about a character; a description or representation of a person's qualities or peculiarities.

Classify: To arrange according to a category or trait.

Climax: The moment when the action in a story reaches its greatest conflict.

Compare and contrast: To examine the likenesses and differences of two people, ideas or things. (*Contrast* always emphasizes differences. *Compare* may focus on likenesses alone or on likenesses and differences.)

Conflict: The main source of drama and tension in a literary work; the discord between persons or forces that brings about dramatic action.

Connotation: Something suggested or implied, not actually stated.

Description: An account that gives the reader a mental image or picture of something.

Dialect: A form of language used in a certain geographic region; it is distinguished from the standard form of the language by pronunciation, grammar and/or vocabulary.

Dialogue (dialog): The parts of a literary work that represent conversation.

Fact: A piece of information that can be proven or verified.

Figurative language: Description of one thing in terms usually used for something else. Simile and metaphor are examples of figurative language.

Flashback: The insertion of an earlier event into the normal chronological sequence of a narrative.

Foreshadowing: The use of clues to give readers a hint of events that will occur later on.

Historical fiction: Fiction represented in a setting true to the history of the time in which the story takes place.

Imagery: Language that appeals to the senses; the use of figures of speech or vivid descriptions to produce mental images.

Irony: The use of words to express the opposite of their literal meaning.

Legend: A story handed down from earlier times; its truth is popularly accepted but cannot be verified.

Limerick: A humorous five-lined poem with a specific form: aabba. Lines 1, 2 and 5 are longer than lines 3 and 4.

Metaphor: A figure of speech that compares two unlike things without the use of like or as.

Mood: The feeling that the author creates for the reader.

Motivation: The reasons for the behavior of a character.

Narrative: The type of writing that tells a story.

Narrator: The character who tells the story.

Opinion: A personal point of view or belief.

Parody: Writing that ridicules or imitates something more serious.

Personification: A figure of speech in which an inanimate object or an abstract idea is given human characteristics.

Play: A literary work that is written in dialogue form and that is usually performed before an audience.

Plot: The arrangement or sequence of events in a story.

Point of view: The perspective from which a story is told.

Protagonist: The main character.

Pun: A play on words that are similar in sound but different in meaning.

Realistic fiction: True-to-life fiction; the people, places and happenings are similar to those in real life.

Resolution: The part of the plot from the climax to the ending where the main dramatic conflict is worked out.

Satire: A literary work that pokes fun at individual or societal weaknesses.

Sequencing: The placement of story elements in the order of their occurrence.

Setting: The time and place in which the story occurs.

Simile: A figure of speech that uses *like* or *as* to compare two unlike things.

Stereotype: A character whose personality traits represent a group rather than an individual.

Suspense: Quality that causes readers to wonder what will happen next.

Symbolism: The use of a thing, character, object or idea to represent something else.

Synonyms: Words that are very similar in meaning.

Tall tale: An exaggerated story detailing unbelievable events.

Theme: The main idea of a literary work; the message the author wants to communicate, sometimes expressed as a generalization about life.

Tone: The quality or feeling conveyed by the work; the author's style or manner of expression.

ANSWERS

Pre-Reading Activity: Civil War Beginnings
1. 11   2. 24, if you include West Virginia

Pre-Reading Activity: Major Battles of the Civil War
NOTE: Not all of the following information is included in the novel.

Fort Sumter (April 12-13, 1861)—Confederate General P.G.T. Beauregard demanded surrender of Fort Sumter, South Carolina, but Major Anderson refused. Confederates fired upon the fort. On April 14 Anderson surrendered. The firing upon Fort Sumter marked the start of the war.

The First Battle of Bull Run, or Manassas (July 21, 1861)—Confederates under General Beauregard stopped the Union assault led by General Irvin McDowell and counterattacked. Union troops retreated to Washington.

The Second Battle of Bull Run, or Manassas (August 29-30, 1862)—Union troops under Major General John Pope attacked Confederate forces led by General "Stonewall" Jackson. General Robert E. Lee arrived and halted the assault. Union troops were driven back.

Pittsburg Landing, or Shiloh (April 6-7, 1862)—Confederates led by General A.S. Johnston took Union troops led by General Ulysses S. Grant by surprise at Shiloh, Tennessee, near Pittsburg Landing. General Johnston was killed in battle and General Beauregard took command. General Grant's troops received reinforcements led by General Buell. Union troops regained their original lines and the Confederates withdrew to Corinth, Mississippi, an important Confederate railroad and communications center. After Shiloh, General Halleck came to Pittsburg Landing and took Corinth, gaining control of this important position; however, many considered this to be an empty victory, for General Beauregard had already abandoned this position.

Antietam Creek (September 17, 1862)—Confederate troops in Western Maryland under General Lee had been divided, but General McClellan gave Lee enough time to pull his army together behind Antietam Creek. McClellan made several powerful attacks, but when General Stonewall Jackson arrived with reinforcements, McClellan was overcautious and called off the battle. Lee retreated to Virginia. McClellan waited before following him, thereby failing to take advantage of the situation. This is said to be the bloodiest single-day battle of the war.

Fredericksburg (December 13, 1861)—General Ambrose Burnside marched Union troops numbering about 120,000 to a point across the river from Fredericksburg, Virginia. He then ordered a series of hopeless assaults against General Lee's Confederate forces of about 78,000. Burnside lost 12,653; Lee lost 5,309. Union morale plummeted. Burnside was replaced.

Chancellorsville (May 1-5, 1863)—General Lee's Confederate troops beat General Hooker's Union troops at Chancellorsville, Virginia; however, Lee's ablest general, General "Stonewall" Jackson, was fatally wounded; this was a great loss to the South.

Gettysburg (July 1-3, 1863)—On the third day of this battle General Lee sent about 15,000 Confederate troops to attack Cemetery Ridge, which was held by about 10,000 Federals, or Union troops. They penetrated the ridge but could do no more. On July 4 Lee retreated from Pennsylvania to Virginia. Union General Meade has been criticized for not pursuing the enemy; nevertheless, Lee never again was able to mount a full-scale invasion. Gettysburg is considered by many to be a turning point in the war.

Vicksburg (May 1863)—General Grant's Federal troops closed in on Vicksburg, Mississippi, and lay siege for 6 weeks. General Pemberton finally surrendered on July 4. As a result, the Union achieved an important strategic goal: control of the Mississippi River. The Confederacy was now split in half. This was probably the most important turning point of the war.

Chattanooga (November 23-25, 1863)—After their defeat at Chickamauga Creek, Tennessee, Union troops were able to make an orderly withdrawal to nearby Chattanooga. General Bragg eventually advanced on Chattanooga, but General Grant was able to break the siege. This was an important victory for the Federals because they kept control of this important rail center and were again in a position to split the Confederacy.

Atlanta (May 1863)—General William T. Sherman, commander of the Western army, was to march into northern Georgia and destroy the Confederate army, which was led by General Joseph E. Johnston, and to destroy the economic resources of Atlanta. As Sherman neared Atlanta, Johnston was replaced by the more aggressive General Hood. Hood launched 2 unsuccessful attacks against Sherman. Atlanta fell into Union hands on September 2. From there, Sherman set out on his great March to the Sea that lay waste to the economic resources of Georgia.

Chapter One: Vocabulary

1. accustomed	3. amiable	5. caress	7. radiance, dissipate	9. secession	11. physics
2. destiny	4. melancholy, typhoid	6. imminence	8. alleged, aloof	10. apathy	12. tariffs

Chapter One: Comprehension and Discussion Questions (Answers may vary.)

1. He thought that it was unmanly to fear war. He thought war was exciting and was anxious for war to begin. "He liked to hear stories of war. . . . He was one with young Tom and Eb when they hoped that war would come soon. . . . War meant loud brass music and shining horses. . . uniforms finer than any suit. . . ." He knew war meant death, but he didn't think anyone he knew would be among the fallen.

2. Shad was going to try to get more news of the impending war.

3. He admired both men and had confidence in both of them; however, he was also somewhat angry at both of them: his father for not punishing Travis Burdow and President Lincoln for wavering about the war.

4. Answers will vary, but some might guess that Bill will fight on the side of the Confederates. "Bill, for the first time that John could remember, had reservations about a subject and seemed unwilling to discuss it with his brother. . . . There was a silence in the air."

Chapter Two: Comprehension and Discussion Questions (Answers may vary.)

1. He said that slavery had always existed and that even the founding fathers recognized the institution of slavery.

2. He was beginning to have some doubts. He tried to understand the true meaning of war, but was frustrated by his inability to do so.

3. Wilse Graham: Wilse will probably be on the side of the Confederates. ''The South asks only to be left alone.'' ''The high-tariff industrialists would sooner hev the South starve than give an inch that might cost them a penny.''
John: John will probably be on the side of the Union. ''What about the right and wrong of one man ownin' the body...of another man?'' ''Only to be left alone to carry slavery into every new territory...to spread the shame of this land.''
Bill: Bill seems to be leaning toward the Southern view. ''We're from the South, John; would we want men of their kind tellin' us how we must live?''

4. Shad told them that the Confederates had fired on Fort Sumter. This was important because it meant the start of the war.

Chapter Three: Vocabulary

1. H	4. F	7. O	10. D	13. E	16. N
2. L	5. A	8. B	11. Q	14. P	17. K
3. M	6. I	9. C	12. J	15. G	

Chapter Three: Comprehension and Discussion Questions (Answers may vary.)

1. People traveled to different towns to hear the speeches. There were were picnics and brass bands.

2. Many realized that the predictions of an early, easy victory were not going to come true. There were ''no more confident statements of ending the whole affair in one decisive swoop.''

3. ''He no longer talked to the children [who were buried there] though; a phase of innocence had passed, which would never be recaptured.''

4. He told Jeth that he was leaving and that he would fight for the South. As Bill walked away, Jethro hid his face because of a superstition he had heard from his mother: If you watch a loved one leave for a long journey, it will be the last time you see him.

Chapter Four: Vocabulary

1. warnings	4. scatter	7. swirled pattern	9. reprimand	11. doubt	13. compassionate
2. hint	5. manipulate	8. self-important	10. contempt	12. seriously	14. shyly
3. ominously	6. imitation				

Chapter Four: Comprehension and Discussion Questions (Answers may vary.)

1. They rang in celebration of the victories at Fort Henry and Fort Donelson.

2. She suggested that he visit Shad.

3. Jethro said that Jenny, whom Shad wanted to marry, was a bit young. Shad felt somewhat betrayed by someone he thought would be on his side; therefore, he made a literary reference to Julius Caesar's exclamation to Brutus for taking part in his murder.

4. He wanted Jeth to live with him and Jenny and to go to a fine university. Shad left Jethro his books to read. He advised him to read all he could and to study the newspapers, even if he found it difficult.

Chapter Five: Comprehension and Discussion Questions (Answers may vary.)

1. He was proud that his father trusted him to handle the difficult job. ''To cover that distance with a team, to do the chores and handle money—that was a man's job. To be trusted with it was a huge satisfaction.''

2. Answers might vary, but he respected Jeth for standing up for his brother and felt badly that Jeth had encountered such ill feelings. He gave Jeth a book about correct speech.

3. Answers might vary, but he probably was grateful to Matt for sparing his son although his son was responsible for Matt's daughter's death.

4. Jethro probably didn't want to upset them. Answers will vary, but it was probably in their best interests to be aware of what was going on.

Chapter Six: Comprehension and Discussion Questions (Answers may vary.)

1. He didn't ask about the war news anymore. He praised his younger children. ''The older children of the family would have been surprised.''

2. Thousands of Union soldiers had died at Pittsburg Landing (Shiloh). They worried that Tom or Eb might have been among them.

3. The difference in their ages no longer seemed so great. Jethro had become more of a peer. Jenny knew how much Jethro had wanted to read Shad's letter. She offered to let him read it although it was very personal. Jeth had matured, however, and realized—after having discussed the matter with Nancy—that it would not be right for him to read what was meant only for Jenny. He was mature enough to respect her privacy.

4. There were some who held it against the entire family that Bill had joined the Confederates in spite of the fact that his other sons were fighting for the Union.

Chapter Seven: Vocabulary

1. I	4. B	7. M	10. L	13. F
2. O	5. A	8. N	11. E	14. H
3. G	6. C	9. D	12. J	15. K

Chapter Seven: Comprehension and Discussion Questions (Answers may vary.)

1. Answers will vary, but the Creightons were told about Tom's death by Dan Lawrence, who gave a sympathetic, eyewitness account.

2. An addendum was about to be added—the time and place of Tom's death—just as it had been added to the listings of his brothers and sister who had died previously.

3. General Beauregard had withdrawn his troops; Halleck had captured a deserted town.

4. According to Jethro, the problem was the Union generals. " 'And how does it happen. . .that the Lord lets Jeff Davis get men like Lee and Jackson and gives us ones like McClellan and Halleck?' "

Chapter Eight: Comprehension and Discussion Questions (Answers may vary.)

1. Two Confederate generals, Bragg and Smith, had driven the Federals out of the Cumberland Gap in Tennessee. Also, Confederate generals, Stonewall Jackson and Robert E. Lee, had scored a victory in Virginia. This news was surprising to Jethro because—like others in the North—his hopes had been raised and he thought that the North was winning the war.

2. In Chapter 5 Ross Milton had given Jethro a book to help him improve his grammar. He was glad that Jethro had gained from it.

3. Answers will vary, but most will probably say that he was an excellent, motivating leader. If they take Shad's word for it, they will probably add that his desire to be liked and his fear for having his men die in battle interfered with his desire to win the war at all costs.

4. He compared General Burnside and the other leaders involved with the Battle of Fredericksburg to murderers because they knew that there would be little chance for success. He called it a "cruel, futile battle." He believed Burnside to be cruel, stubborn, and self-righteous.

Chapter Nine: Vocabulary

1. bachelor	3. faltering	5. triumphant	7. credence	9. ventured	11. gangrenous
2. suspicion	4. decline	6. ancestral	8. conscience	10. despairing	12. insistence

Chapter Nine: Comprehension and Discussion Questions (Answers may vary.)

1. Hig Phillips was a draft dodger. He was a lazy bachelor who did not want to fight in the war, so he paid three hundred dollars for a substitute. He was killed by deserters who resented his indifference.

2. Jenny was angry that the men had barged into their home, assuming that they were hiding Eb. She made them feel uncomfortable. "It is easier to come to a house and upset a sick old man and scared womenfolk," she said.

3. He weighed the pros and cons. Against him helping were the possibility of getting the family in trouble with the law; loyalty to Tom and the others who had given their lives; and the thought of the consequences should more and more soldiers decide to quit. In favor of helping was the desire not to be responsible for sending his cousin to his death and not wanting to see him living like a hunted animal. He asked Eb if he would be willing to go back if given the chance. When Eb said that he would, Jeth decided to help him in the only way he knew. He wrote a letter to President Lincoln and let Eb stay while he waited for a response.

4. Answers will vary. (Lincoln had ordered that all deserters who reported by April 1 be returned to their regiments without punishment except forfeiture of pay.)

Chapter Ten: Vocabulary

1. advantaged	3. monotonous	5. optimism	7. conspiracy	9. maneuvered	11. verified
2. arrogant	4. spinster	6. dreary	8. seize	10. contemptuous	12. inept

Chapter Ten: Comprehension and Discussion Questions (Answers may vary.)

1. Joe Hooker had entered the battle with superior numbers of soldiers but had failed miserably.

2. Many people wanted President Lincoln to get rid of Grant. Although at first they admired him for the victories at Fort Henry and Fort Donelson, they later said that he should not be given credit for them. There were rumors of drunkenness. Although the rumors were not verified, those who had lost family members and friends under Grant's command were aroused to anger by the stories. Robert E. Lee, on the other hand, had become a legend. He seemed to be unbeatable. He was very well respected.

3. Ross volunteered to accompany Jenny to Washington, D.C., when they learned that Shad had been critically wounded. Matt probably would not have let Jenny travel alone. This is evidenced by the fact that he agreed that Ross should go even though Ross was ill.

4. Jenny made the best of a difficult situation. Although her aunt objected at first, Jenny insisted on going to the hospital to help those who were suffering. Things that in the past would have made her faint, she confronted with courage. Although there were many discomforts, she was happy just to be by her husband's side.

Chapter Eleven: Comprehension and Discussion Questions (Answers may vary.)

1. According to John, the battle was important because after the Union soldiers had conquered Missionary Ridge, thereby breaking the middle of the Confederate line, General Bragg was forced to retreat. John was proud that the Army of the Cumberland had accomplished this feat.

2. Lincoln's Proclamation of Amnesty gave full rights to any Confederate soldier who would swear to protect the Constitution and the Union and who would abide by the laws against slavery. This meant Bill would be safe from punishment.

3. Shad was for Lincoln, but although he had blamed McClellan for the great losses at Antietam, he also saw in him great courage that he had to cheer for.

4. If Bill was not at Pittsburg Landing, he could not have been the one to kill Tom.

Chapter Twelve: Comprehension and Discussion Questions (Answers may vary.)

1. Sherman burned farms and destroyed the countryside on his march from Atlanta to the sea. People learned of the destruction and reacted differently. Some felt the rebels just got what they deserved for trying to destroy the Union. Others felt badly, but thought this type of action would help put an end to the war. Still others felt that the looting, arson, and violence aimed at civilians was unnecessary and that even war should have limits.

2. Answers will vary.

3. Ross said, "Don't expect peace to be a perfect pearl" because he welcomed peace, but he knew that the problems were not over. The physical destruction could be handled, but the emotional scars left by a civil war would be harder to heal. "It's a far star...a dim pinpoint in the light in the darkness" referred to the thirteenth amendment and the abolition of slavery. He worried that the freed slaves would not be able to adapt to their new freedom and that they would be uneducated and easily exploited.

4. People were overjoyed at the prospect of peace. Their feelings changed from elation to great despair when they learned of the assassination of President Lincoln.

Spotlight Literary Skill: Mood

1. sorrowful, despairing   2. joyous, exciting

3. sad, fearful, serious, apprehensive   4. apprehensive, tense, suspenseful   5. happy, optimistic

Crossword Puzzle:

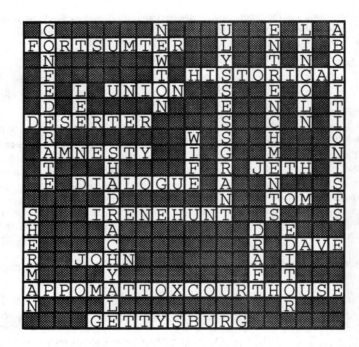

© 1995 Educational Impressions, Inc.